Self help
How to get started

Written by
Simon 'Amazing' Clarke

Edited by
Amy Clarke

Library and Archives Canada Cataloguing in Publication

CIP data on file with the National Library and Archives

ISBN 978-1-55483-916-2

FOREWORD

If you haven't already watched 'The Secret' DVD, or at least read the book. Then you really need to. I could explain here what 'The Secret' is, or how it works, but I won't.

Basically it would take me half the book to explain what the 'The Secret' is all about, but as Rhonda Byrne and the team have done such a fantastic job, then you really need to watch it, or read it for yourself.

What I will say is, all of our thoughts and actions have brought us to where we are now. Our future thoughts and actions will change our lives, in ways that we will find almost unrecognisable.

This is what happened to me. I started writing this book at a time in my life when the biggest changes were starting to happen. It's probably about 6 years since I first watched 'The Secret'.

Since then I have been slowly learning from people like Jack Canfield, 'Chicken Soup For The Soul' & 'How To Get From Where You Are To Where You Want To Be', Neale Donald Walshe 'Conversations with God' and Joe Vitale 'The Attraction Factor'.

Each of these writers has written so many more books, but these are the ones that I know them by. This book isn't designed to replace any of their works, indeed I would hope that after reading my book you will go out and read some of their amazing books.

They have so much more knowledge and experience than I do. They are truly great teachers. That was why they were featured on 'The Secret'.

As is usual in a foreword I'd like to take a moment to thank a few people who have helped me get to this place in my life.

I'd like to thank Mark and Claire Doyle for getting me started on this journey of self-enrichment. I'd like to thank Andrew Danyardi for his amazing powers and his insistence that I watch 'The Secret'. I'd also like to thank Gary and Diane Howarth and Janet Varley for their years of friendship and support.

If we are talking about great teachers in life, I must mention my Parents. They not only brought me into this world and formed me into the person that I was, but they were also open minded enough to change with me and become all that they wanted to be. So I'd like to take this opportunity to thank my parents Peter and Brenda Clarke for being who they are.

Thanks must also go to my long-suffering Daughter, Amy Clarke. She has been with me throughout all of my changes. She not only benefited from my financial and spiritual changes but she also excelled from the changes within her too.

Throughout this book I refer to the things that I have done. This is not impress you, it is to impress upon you the things that you can do. Don't be limited by the words that I write. You can push your personal envelope wherever you like.

Just as an example, my parents didn't start scuba diving until they were in there 70's!

If you are not getting as much from
your life as you want to,
Then examine the state of your enthusiasm.
Norman Vincent Peale 1898-1993

TABLE OF CONTENTS

Chapter 1

LETS GET STARTED

This book contains stories and information that I have come across over the last few years. I like to think that I have a really good memory and I must state here quite clearly, that if there is something I have got, not quite right then, it is a memory problem on my part.

The information contained in this book is intended to help you. It's like the information you get from a close friend. Information, is one thing, it's up to you what you do with it. I know what I have done with the information that I have got from the books that I have read. I've used it to help me move forward and I've also used it to help those around me.

This is the same information that I have passed on to my parents, my friends and even my Daughter.

As I mentioned before, I got started about 6 years ago. I sort of knew about the Self-help market and I kept think to myself that maybe I ought to read one of these books. To be honest, at the time, it was a choice between a magazine, the TV or the pub.

You can see where I was in my life.

Some people think that self-help Books are a modern phenomenon. You will see by some of the quotes that I have in this book that it goes back hundreds of years.

Believe that life is worth living,
And you belief will help create the fact.
William James 1842-1910

Here is something that will astound you. Here's a quote from 2000 years ago.

The Universe is transformation.
Our life is what out thoughts make it.
Marcus Aurelius 121 - 180

You see, there is nothing new about having information that can, and will, change your life. As you find out in 'The Secret', it's been kept from us. That's why it all seems so new.

The reality is, there are only few things you need to do to change your life.

They are not difficult and they will not take long to do. The difficult bit, and the one that can take you the time, is learning how to do it. This is what my book is all about.

Before we get onto that, let me offer you a couple of choices.

Would you prefer to: -

A, Read 50+ books (some of which might, or might not help you)?

Or

B, Read some books that I recommend that will start to change your life quicker?

If your anything like me, you will choose the easier option. It is, after all, Human nature and what got us to where we are.

The details I give here and the books that I recommend are not an exhaustive list. They are here as a help to getting you started. Because all of us are different, and as I don't know your personality or circumstances, I can't recommend too many books to you. All I can do, and all that I intend to do, is to get you started on the path to enlightenment.

The Power of the written word, now there is an interesting little comment.

It's interesting, we all learned to read when we were at school, but how many of us have ever come across powerful phrases and stories.

I'll tell you, I was amazed. I didn't come across anything like this until I was in my late 30's.

Later on in the book I will be asking you to write down your goals and dreams.

There is something I need to tell you. This is your Book. Whether you bought it, or someone gave it too you, it's the same thing.

You are encouraged, with self-help books to write in them, highlight them, turn the corner of the pages, and add sticky notes.

You can do anything you like to it, because it is yours.

As children, we were told that books are precious and we should take care of them. This isn't a book; it's your future.

Chapter 2

THE DIFFERENCES BETWEEN US

We often wonder why some people can do things and others can't. Why some people are more out going and why some have endless patients. There is always the big question about the differences between Men and Women.

It's strange, I've actually never read 'Men are from Mars and Women are from Venus'. I have heard that it's a great book.

However, I used to have an audio book that was similar to that but by a different Author. Unfortunately their name escapes me. But both of these works explain basically the same thing. Men and Women are wired differently.

When a Man says something to a Woman and she doesn't understand, it's because she doesn't understand. The opposite is also true.

What is important to one, is not important to the other. It's not because they don't care or they are not interested, it's because they genuinely don't understand.

Fact, Men and Women are wired differently. Don't believe me. Guys, go and multi-task. Girls, point to north.

For a guy to understand a woman he has to think like a woman. Now I know at first thought you will be thinking 'yeah, like that's ever going to happen'. Well actually it can, and Women can learn to think like men. If two people in a relationship can learn how the other thinks, it makes life a lot easier and more fun.

The other thing to work out is your personality Style. They're a many ways of categorising our selves. The one that I learned, which I find easy to pick up and a really great help to understanding me, and the people that I meet, is DISC.

By asking, or thinking about two easy question, we can work our, or someone else's, personality.

I know that this simple test can make an instant difference to your life. Get yourself a copy of 'Sponsor With Style' by Robert Rohm.

Although it is basically a book to help Network marketers, the DISC system helps everyone.

So why is important to understand how Men and Women are different and what other people personalities are? There are two simple answers.

1, You get to understand who you are.

2, Moving forward in life usually involves interacting with more people.

If you want to make more money, then you need to get along with other people better. In a later chapter I will tell you a story about a guy who sold gym equipment and because he work with the differences and personalities made a very nice living.

Chapter 3

SETTING GOALS

I have read a great many books over the last 10 to 15 years. In this book I intend to impart some of that knowledge to you. I have read from such great Authors as Susan Jeffers, Jack Canfield and John Maxwell.

There are a few common themes that I want to touch on now that I have read in several books. There are three big ones.

1, Dream big and you can have what you want out of life.
   To help you achieve this you need to follow

2, Make a list of your Dreams and Goals

3, Read that list daily and do things that will help you achieve them.

I have followed these three rules over the years, since I was introduced to 'The Secret'. I suppose this is where my successes have come from.

Unfortunately, I have followed rule 1 really well, and rules 2 & 3 only a little bit. I think, this answers my question, why I have not achieved all of the goals that I have wanted to. That is partially (or mainly) because I didn't have a clear vision of what I want to achieve.

Having said that, I do know what I want. I want a big win on the Lottery. Well, big enough so that I don't have to work. I don't want to be greedy; $1,000,000 would do for starters. Actually that would be great, but not totally life changing.

Well, it could be I suppose. So I really need $2,000,000 to get me set up.

Thinking about it $5,000,000 would be a better figure. I wouldn't have to work, I can do what I want, give what I want to my family and friends and help out Charities.

If I want to help charities as well over my life time I'd better start by wanting to win $10,000,000.

Do you see my problem!

I needed some clear set goals of what I want, and work each and every day towards achieving them. My goals need to be 100% defined so that I can focus like a laser on getting there. A Laser is an electronic device that concentrates light, that is shooting of in all direction, and concentrates it into a singular beam of focused energy.

If you, and I, focus on our goals like that, we will get there.

A year ago I had a picture of Toronto taken from the CN Tower as my wallpaper on my PC. It was just a random picture I found on the Internet. At that time I wanted to move and work abroad, but I didn't know where I wanted to move too.

3 months later I moved to Toronto to a job that came totally out of the Blue. 3 months after that I was seated in that restaurant.

Set your sights high, the higher the better.
Expect the most wonderful things to happen,
not in the future but now.
Realize that nothing is too good.
Allow absolutely nothing to hamper you
or hold you up in any way.
Eileen Caddy – Co-Founder of the Findhorn Foundation

Getting back to rules 2 & 3, I need every effort I can to focus on my goals, by doing that I know, I will achieve what I want.

How am I so sure? Because it has worked for other people and I have made it work for me. Let me give you another example. A few years ago I had a part time business that sold energy drinks. We used to do promotions at sporting events. 10k runs were particularly good.

As I stood at my stand talking to runners and their family's promoting our wares, I was in total awe of the people who could run 10k's, that's over 6 miles.

I'd been going to the Gym for a while by this stage. So I was getting fitter although I still weighted over 18st (250 lbs+). I did find that I was starting to enjoy the running.

Well, to the amazement of everyone, including my self, I increased my distance until I was able to run a 10k on the treadmill. I immediately booked myself in for a 10k run for the following month.

I was there to run and not compete so I started at the back and successful held onto my place. I ran all the way around and even passed a few people on the way.

I was over come with emotion as I passed the finishing line. I'd achieved what I had set out to complete. I'd run a 10k road race and finished in just under an hour. I think it was actually my best time for a 10k too.

I mention later on in this book how my job and life changed because of the books I had read. I decided one time to find my self and executive car. I didn't really know what I wanted but I did come across pictures of a classic 7 Series BMW. It was pictured with a beautiful V8 and Leather seats. It was gorgeous. It was about 15 years old, but in excellent condition. The big engine purred when you started her up. Not only did I buy this car, but I also got it at a price below the original asking price. Those seats were really comfortable. They had heaters to so you could warm your bum on cold mornings.

Another time I was out for a ride on my motorbike when I had a thought to take a look around the local Nissan Dealership. There was a relatively new car style at the time in the UK called the Qashqai. I had a look around them and had a chat to one of the sales guys. To cut a long story short, I ordered a brand new one and within a few months I was driving around the sort of car that I never thought I could have had or afforded.

Both of these things I didn't think that I could own, but within months of wanting them, they arrived in my life.

Chapter 4

YOUR JOURNEY BEGINS

Retirement isn't about being old, broke and shuffling around in your slippers. It's about having the time, money and health to do those fun things in life that you have always wanted to.

We should all have a bucket list, a list of all the things you want to do before you kick the bucket. The name is quite obvious really, but do you know many people who have such a list?

Write one, write it now. Go on; write down 10 things that you would love to do. You can call it a 'wish list' if you want or a 'to do' list. The important thing is that you write a list. I've done this several times and it's amazing how it works.

> *Shoot for the Moon. Even if you miss it,*
> *you will land among the stars.*
> Lester Louis Brown b. 1928

I'll give you a bit of a clue here. Do the things in your life that you want to do, when you are capable of doing them. Don't get to 90 years old in an old folk's home and 'Wish' that you had done these things.

I wrote on my first wish list that I wanted to Swim with Sharks (don't ask, it's a Scuba diver thing). I wanted to record a CD, (no, I wasn't singing) and I wanted to go to Jamaica. There were a few other things on that list but I moved 6 months later and the list never went back up. Thinking about it, I didn't complete everything on that list.

Within a few months I'd done those three and a couple more from my list. The Holiday in Jamaica I'll describe later. The Scuba Diving with Sharks was amazing and the recording the CD. Well can you imagine what it was like spending the day with self made millionaires talking about their product lines?

The simple clue here is, write it down and make it happen. You will be amazed what comes true when you write a list of things you want to do. Thinks just pop into your life unexpectedly.

There is a great book called 'Write It Down And Make It Happen' by Henriette Klauser.

Not only does she relate some great stories of how people have changed their lives by using a variety of great but simple techniques; she does it in a way that makes the book hard to put down.

Let me describe your life to you in another way. Again it's an easy A or B choice.

Plan A – Work from 18 to 65 (+) and retire broke!
Plan B – Work from 18 till 5 years from now and retire to a fun life!

The choice is yours, the power is in your hands, all you have to do is believe in yourself.

Dream what you want to dream,
Go where you want to go,
Be what you want to be.
Because you have only one life,
And only one chance,
To do all of the things you want to do.

Unknown

This is not all about the money. Its about happiness, better relationships and less stress

When you wake up in the morning do you want to jump out of bed regardless of what the time is?

Or do you struggle to get up in the morning and drag your self to a job that you don't like and doesn't pay well.

Of those two, which would you rather have?

It's important to remember that life is here to be enjoyed and not to be a struggle. You should be living a life where you smile every day. The biggest thing for me is being able to do what I want, when I want and having the money to be able to do it.

If we did all of the things
We are capable of doing,
We would truly astound ourselves

Thomas Edison 1847-1931

Chapter 5

READ AND LEARN

Within the books that I have read there are stories that have really inspired me.

I have also included stories of things that have happened to me, my friends and my family. Stories where a positive, purposeful and consistent mindset has produces incredible results.

These results continue, as long as I put in the consistent effort.

I have a dream to teach people what I know and what I know worked for me. I teach what I have learned from 'The Secret', Jack Canfield, Joe Vitale and others.

I achieved this even though I haven't had any teacher training and no high academic qualifications in this field. Actually looking at my qualifications, it's quite surprising I achieved anything in my life.

But I have. Why, because I have put in the consistent effort when others doubted me and thought that my ideas were fanciful.

I am a guy who didn't do very well at school but since then I have listened and learned. Don't do like me and take 5 years plus to make these changes. Read and act upon what you read.

Ok so time for a reality check, you won't change you life today, you won't change your life tomorrow, but you will start to change your life.

In his book 'How To Write And Publish Your Own EBook In As Little As 7 Days' Joe Vitale describes how you can actually do that. Write and publish an ebook in only 7 day. So, theoretically you can publish your book in 7 days and receive your first pay cheque within a month. 6 months down the line, it might be possible for you to retire on an income that is higher than your current salary. Now, does that blow your brain or what?

That would take dedication and a lot of hard work, but it is achievable.

Great quote, I love this one

The mind is like a parachute
It works better when it's open

Frank Zappa

Well here's the thing, unless you do something about it, put the rubber to the road so to speak, you won't achieve anything.

If you follow the action plans out lined here and in the books I recommend, you WILL change you life for the better. It's worked for me and it has worked for millions of other people too.

I will tell you tales of ordinary worker Joe, people who have done amazing things. What special skills did they have when they started? None. They were no different to you or I.

Within 6 months, they changed their lives. Sometimes from the outside in 6 months it's obvious what the changes are. Sometimes it's not.

For me, nothing much seemed to happen for the first 4 years. But underneath they were. It's only years later that you realize where the changes are occurring.

It takes 5 years to become and overnight success

Let's do it quicker than that and prove people wrong.

I say this because in a few months, if you are following my advice, and the other authors mentioned in this book and you think nothing is happening, relax and trust me that it is.

Fortunately your success is not necessarily related to your qualifications from school. I can't remember the exact figure but it's something like 75% of all self-made millionaires were only 'C' grade students. I feel very lucky. I was a 'C' grade student.

> *Genius is one percent inspiration*
> *And ninety-nine percent perspiration*
> Thomas Edison 1847-1931

I feel very privileged to live when I do. So much information is available if only we are prepared to look, and do something about it.

Chapter 6

INTO THE BOOKS

I've already mentioned 'The Secret' a few times already, I can't stress how important it is to watch the DVD or read the book. The first time you are introduced to 'The Secret' you will be blown away.

'The Secret' introduces you to a lot of people. I have got to know a few of these over the last few years and I want to introduce them to you. Before I get too much into this, I want to repeat the purpose of this book.

You have many choices in life. Go to any bookstore, or on-line store and pick for yourself some self-help / motivational books.

This is not always a great success. I've bought books that didn't really help. On the other hand sometimes this has really worked for me. I can be browsing the self-help section in a bookstore, when I seem drawn to a particular book.

They can turn out to be good books. Unfortunately, sometimes I can pick up a book that either I didn't connect with, or didn't have the sort of information that I wanted, or I'd already come across before.

In 'The Secret', Rhonda Byrne introduces us to a great many teachers including Bob Doyle, Jack Canfield, Joe Vitale and Bob Proctor. In addition to these people, there is something like another 20 to 30 people that get introduced. I haven't yet read anything by these people so I won't be commenting on them in this book.

I have read a lot of Jack Canfield books, you may have noticed by now that I mention his name a lot. Jack has teamed up with a number of other top Authors in many of his books and book series. Follow the links at the back of this book for more information on them and his co-authors and for all of the Authors mentioned in this book.

The first book that I want to mention is 'How To Get From Where You Are To Where You Want To Be'. I mention this book else where in my book for good reason, it worked for me.

Jack has done an updated and expanded version of the original book that I have bought. The new one is called 'The Success Principles' and it contains even more great tip, ideas and ways of changing your life. I have both books, both are brilliant and both are life changers. Pick one and read it.

If I were to recommend one of these for you, I'd probably pick 'How To Get From Where You Are To Where You Want To Be'. It's shorter than 'Success Principles'. If you are not a big reader, I'd say it's a bit easier to get through. Very important thought is to remember to do the actions that you are told to do. I know I keep on saying the same things throughout this book (there is a reason for that too). The important part is not the reading, but the doing.

One of the greatest series of books that I have ever read is the 'Chicken Soup for the Soul'. It really is a strange title but you must read the original one first then look for the rest of the series. I've read, probably half a dozen 'Chicken Soup for the Soul' books including the one for 'Country and Westerns Soul' and 'Ocean Souls'.

These books will really move you. They contain totally amazing stories about what people have done, have achieved and, as important, what people have done for others.

A big tip here with the 'Chicken Soup for the Soul' series of books, have a box of tissues handy. They really pull at the heart strings.

Let me give you a couple of stories to read. 'The Royal Knights of Harlem' and the story of John Goddard. Both of these stories will let you look at other people with different eyes and help you believe that you can achieve anything you want in your life.

The 'The Royal Knights of Harlem' is the Story of an ordinary set of high school kids who had amazing achievements, with of all things, a Chess board!

The big 'But' here thought is, that after they left school and with the experiences that they had, they went onto even greater things.

John Goddard is someone to inspire everyone. Write a list and make it happen. Reading this story will change your outlook completely.

Some men see things as they are and say 'Why'?
I dream things that never were and say 'Why not?'
George Bernard Shaw 1856-1950

The third book of Jacks that I want to recommend is 'You Have Got To Read This Book' it is an amazing collection of stories how books changed peoples lives. When I first read that book, I was so inspired that I bought and read some of the books that were mentioned in it. From each one I learned something, grew and moved on.

Jack has many books out there for you to read and learn from. The last one that I want to recommend for now is the 'Aladdin Factor'. This is a book you really want to learn from.

Another book series that I enjoyed reading and was also from one of the teachers on 'The Secret' and really expanded my mind was Neale Donald Walsch's 'Conversations with God'. I remember the first time I heard the tittle of this book I was skeptical. At that point in my life, anytime I heard or say the word 'God'; it made me want to avoid it. They really are amazing books.

Neale had been really down on his luck and was eventually homeless. This book started when he wanted to write a letter of complain but he didn't know who to write it to, so he complained to God. When he finished writing, his pen kept on moving.......

Chapter 7

WHAT IS THE WEALTH THAT YOU SEEK?

Let's stop here for a moment. Wherever you are in your life, you want more (Otherwise you would not be reading the book). But, your outlook on life is limited by where you are in life. Don't worry, I've been there. I've got the hat and the 'T' Shirt.

I am going to say something now; from 'The Magic Of Thinking Big' by David Schwartz you need to think bigger. You might think that it would be nice to own a nice car, but your thought of a nice car is not good enough. I don't mean that in a bad way, I mean you just need to think bigger.

Let me tell you a few stories about people who became self made millionaires in a relatively short period of time. What did they all have in common? Dreams of great things, but they were also prepared to do something about it and were prepared to put in the hard work.

There is an example in one of the books that I read, I can't remember which one it was in but this guy set up his own home gym equipment business. He make over a million dollars profit in his first year. Totally amazing you might think. Then you ask the question, so, how did he make so much money in one year. The answer is simple he used the same principles that Dale Carnegie teaches. Connect with people, solve their problem and you will make a profit.

This guy would take Gym equipment to people houses for them to try. When the equipment that they ordered arrived, he didn't just deliver the equipment, he's help them set it up, The next part was the clever part, he also help them develop fitness program. He didn't charge them for this, he help them. This simple act helped his business explode.

I have spoken about making money and about Millionaires. The question is, how much money do you want to make? The simple answer is more than you currently are.

Let me describe here the difference between being well of and financially free.

Well off - you are well off you have enough money each month to cover all of your bills and to have some left over. Word of warning here. It's very easy to start spending more than you need to and to hit the credit cards for 'Toys' and over stretching your finances again. Don't, otherwise it is difficult to get to the next stage.

Financially free – there is an interesting story here. A Patent was presented to the US Patent Office. I can't actually remember what the original patent was referring too but there was a paragraph in the middle that defined what being wealthy / financially free was. The definition was quite simple. If you have more money at the end of the month than you did at the beginning of the month and you haven't had to earn that money, then you are rich.

Let's use an extreme example. You have one million dollars in the bank and let's assume that the interest on this is $10,000 a month and you need $8,000 a month to live.

This means that without you doing anything every month your wealth increases.

As another example, in these economic times houses can be bought cheaply. Some time and effort could turn them into rental properties. A cheap rental property will earn you $1,000 a month. If we assume that over a number of years you bought several properties cash and paid for all of the reservations yourself you could have a portfolio of 10 houses. Of the $10,000 from the rental, it would be assumed that you could earn $8,000 a month after fee's etc. If you only needed $6,000 a month to live then your efforts would have made you rich.

These are great examples. I know when I first started out on my journey they were great example but totally out of my league. There was no way that I would have the money to enable me to do things like that.

You can't build a reputation
on what you are going to do.
Henry Ford 1863-1947

The examples above require you to have either a lot of spare cash or have money to invest. So what about people like you and I who don't have money to make investments like that. Here are a couple of amazing stories that did amazing things.

Alcohol in the UK was quite heavily taxed in the early 80's and people in the UK noticed that it was considerably cheaper in the French supermarkets. With the Continent being so close, people would stock up on their way back from holiday with whatever they could carry. People even got to the point of doing 'booze trips' where they would drive to France and back again on the same day just to pick up a carload of booze, especially before Christmas.

With this in mind a couple decided that they could probably make some money out of this. So they rented a lorry trailer, positioned it in a layby on the main road from the French ferry ports to Calais and stocked it with cheap Beer. With having minimal overheads they were able to sell at lower than supermarket prices, but still make a nice profit.

For the first 6 months they lived in the trailer, to make sure that no one stole it. After 6 months their business was booming, they had several trailers, staff and could sleep comfortable at night in proper beds.

Within a couple of years they had a purpose built warehouse that was always stacked high with Beer and other drinks. Their car park was always full. I know, I visited it and bought some beer there.

The next time I saw them they were being interviewed on a UK program that was all about self made millionaires. These days they have a team of people employed to run their business.

The house they were interview in was theirs that they paid cash for and was worth over a million pounds. All because they were prepared to work hard and live in a lorry trailer for 6 months.

The second story from the same TV program is about a lady who lived in Swansea in Wales. This is a lady who made the most of a set of unfortunate circumstances.

Here was a lady who had recently left her Husband and

before we can have what we really want out of life.

You can't cross a wide river in a single leap, but you can cross the same river by simply following the stepping stones.

Don't let your past dictate who you are,
Let it be part of who you will become.
Movie - My Big fat Greek Wedding, 2002

Let me go back a bit to where my personal self-development started. I joined a Network marketing company and became part of a team. This team had a fantastic start up program and continuous education program.

In their start up program I was introduced to such fantastic books as 'How To Win Friends And Influence People' by Dale Carnegie. Carnegie is a name you might have heard of. He was a great entrepreneur. He build companies from nothing and became the richest man of his day. Not bad for an immigrant from Scotland who arrived in America without anything.

The book that was considered to be the next most important, was again an old book, 'The Magic Of Thinking Big' by David Schwarts. In his book he describes how we should set goals and set big ones.

I remember when I first tried setting goals in my life. They were all over the place. In James Arthur Ray's book 'Harmonic Wealth' he mentions several times, people over estimate what they can achieve in one year, yet underestimate what they can achieve in 10 years.

Having said that, it is surprising once you start to get

into the 'groove', just how fast things can start to change. In the summer of 2008 I was on holiday in Egypt and I was reading Jack Canfield's book 'How To Get From Where You Are To Where You Want To Be'. In his book Jack guarantee's that if you follow his advice you will double your income within 2 years.

At the time I thought 'wouldn't that be nice'. As the book I was reading wasn't a first edition he quoted stories that had occurred from earlier editions. There was a story of a lady TV producer who, after reading the book, got a promotion and a 50% pay rise within three months.

As nice as I thought it was, and as much as I wanted it, I didn't think that it would really happen. I really shouldn't have thought so negative because that is precisely what happened to me. I got promoted to head of department and began interviewing and training new team members.

I was so happy in my work; it was like everything was falling into place. The funny thing is, I hadn't started to implement any of Jack's teachings at this stage. The thoughts in my head at that time were, 'what would happen if I did all of the things that Jack Canfield say's to do in his book? Then combine this with other things that the great teachers give in their books. What could I produce in my life and how could I help others do the same'? So the idea for this book was born.

I love to pass on things that I have learned and that have helped me. I live life is a positive way and say 'Amazing' a lot, hence my 'middle' name.

I also love to get people excited about getting more out of their lives.

Getting back to when I realised I was using 'The Secret'.

A couple of things in my life started the slow changes that lead me to where I am now. I remember an incident that happened over 10 years ago. I'd only owned my first house just over a year. As the housing market seemed to be quite buoyant, and it had been a year since I last got it valued, I decided to have it re-valued.

At that time I was earning around £14k a year and with a bit of over time I managed to increase that to £17k.

It turned out that my house had gone up by over £20k. These thoughts wandered around my head. I worked from early morning until the evening 5 days a week missing my family and my house earned more than me. There was something seriously wrong with this picture.

A few years went by and I found my self single, and working 200 miles from home. Either you have been there or you know someone who is going through it. Travelling every weekend. The wonderful motorway, mile after mile. Rain, Snow, Ice and endless traffic jam after endless traffic jam. Oh the joys. I eventually got to one of those turning points.

Through a business decision that I made and the training I started to receive, I started to change and l started to learn a few new skills. No, not like woodwork or weaving. These were important life skills.

It was here that I started to learn phrases like

'If you want to change something in your life,
then you have to change something in your life.

Think about that for a moment. You have been happily going through your life; ok so you moaned and complained a bit, but you never did anything about it did you!

If you are really serious about changing you life (and of those around you that you care about) then you must be prepared to change. Actually I know that you are prepared to change, that's why you bought this book......

The 'you' that is the current you got you to this point in your life. The 'you' that you currently are, will get you no further. To get anymore out of life, you have to be prepared to change.

Don't worry, there is nothing major to the change. Slow and gradual is far better than anything drastic. But you must also be prepared to make these changes each day.

I'm here to help you achieve what you want out of your life the same way that I have achieved and am achieving what I want out of mine.

We haven't failed.
We know a thousand things that won't work,
So we are that much closer to finding what will.
Thomas Edison 1847-1931

Chapter 11

WHAT I LEARNED,
AND WHAT I DIDN'T LISTEN TOO

I'll say that by the time I wrote this book I'd read Forty to Fifty self-help, positive motivation and change your life books.

Did they all work, No!

Was there a good reason why they didn't, Yes? Me….

Am I the reason why I was a failure in life? That's not actually a true statement.

You're only a failure if you give up. It doesn't matter how many times you get knocked down. It's the number of times that you get up.

> *I'm grateful for all of my problems.*
> *As each on of them was overcome*
> *I became stronger and more able*
> *To meet those yet to come.*
> *I grew on my difficulties*
> J. C. Penny 1875 – 1971

Some of the most famous people and some of the wealthiest people, in history and today, have been at the wrong end of life.

They have been in far worse positions than you have.

I suppose the reason why I wasn't having the sort of success that I wanted, was because I wasn't following what the teachers taught.

How many times have you been told to make a list, set goals, decided what it is you want out of life and read them every day? You are told to read them out loud, read them last thing at night and first thing in the morning. Believing positively that you can achieve these things. Many time yes.

All of the other books that I have read, have all said the same thing. Stop reading and start writing. You look around you; there isn't a pen or paper in sight, correct! So you carry on reading. You end the book and feel great. But answer this, have you written down a single goal? No

I mentioned this a couple of chapters ago, have you written your list yet. No, then go and do it now. Yes, Pin it to your Mirror, put it on your desk. Put it on the Fridge. Just put it somewhere where you will notice it every day.

Read it every day.

Sometimes I will admit that I have written goals and they haven't come true, so what's that all that about? Well, that's what this chapter is about. It's about you setting out your life on paper and achieving it. As with all things in life there is a right way and a wrong way.

Always live your life with one dream to fulfil
No matter how many of your dreams you have realized in
the past, always have a dream to go.
Because when you stop dreaming, life becomes a mun-
dane existence.

Sara Henderson 1936-2005

The reason why some of your goals don't come true can be because they are not right for you. Another reason can be that although to begin with you thought that you wanted to do these things, now that your life has moved on, they are not something that you actually want to do any more.

I still haven't achieved one of my goals. That is to drive in a car at 300 mph.

Maybe it's coming, maybe it's not right for me. I don't know, maybe the universe has something different in mind.

Chapter 12

MONEY!

Money can't buy you happiness, but it does give you the giggles. It's easy for people to say that money is not everything, or, money is being materialistic. Well, that is the world in which we live.

To keep the lamp burning
We have to keep putting oil in it.
Mother Teresa of Calcutta 1910-1997

If your washing machine springs a leak and ruins your kitchen floor on the same day that your car breaks down, life is a lot easier if you have money in the bank. I've been there and I know that the Stress that you can have when you have no money to fix even the simple things in life. Life with spare money is not Stress free, but there is a lot, lot less.

I've been in both places, one where there was barely enough money for the essentially in life and where I am now, where all bills are covered and I have money left at the end of the month. I can tell you; it's a far better place than if there is too much month left at the end of the money.

We do have to learn to have money. Suddenly having

too much can be a problem.

It's such an unfortunate fact that for most people, the gift of a large amount of money is actually a bad thing. So many lottery millionaires become broke and bankrupt within the first couple of years.

One of the things that I learned through the process that led me to learning 'The Secret' is that you have to learn about money. When I was first told about this I thought yes, 100 pence equals a pound, five pound notes are blue, 20's are purple, I know all about money.

The trouble is, if you want to accumulate the sort of wealth that I think you do, then you need to learn to live with money. Really, it's like anything in life, you have to learn. You have to crawl before you can walk; you have to drive small engine cars before you can drive big engine cars (insurance companies see to that one).

Here is a great book to help you with this 'Rich Dad, Poor Dad' by Robert Kiyosaki. In this book Robert takes you through his journey learning how money works. You learn from his lessons.

I got the audio book and listened to it in the car. I've gone thought it several times now and learn something new every time. If you are serious about becoming wealthy, then I certainly recommend that you get your self a copy of 'Rich Dad, Poor Dad'.

'The Secret' tells us, that we can have anything that we want. What I would say to you is pace yourself. Yes, you can be retired on 5 times your currently salary in 5 years time, just don't try and do it this year. You need to learn how to use 'The Secret' and you need to learn from the things that the Universe gives you.

Before I started writing this book that is exactly the position I was in. I had opened up my mind to the thought of plenty, the thoughts of unlimited supply. I was now slowly beginning to see the reward and reap the benefits. As always I was thankful for those things which I had been given.

This again is a very important act. You must be thankful for what the Universe has given you so far. Doing that will let the Universe know that you are ready for more.

Be careful with the new responsibilities and set new goals for the next step in my life. The job that I had, that had been lacking in fulfilment, was now bringing me new responsibilities. Greater hours of interesting work and a better hourly rate produced an income that never left me wanting.

What did I do with this extra money? I had more fun, more personal experiences. I also shared it. This is an important lesson. It's not about what you can have; it's about what you have to give. Giving of your time, your money and your energy brings back more of what you have given.

I had been able just a few months before to buy, for the first time in my life, a really nice motorbike instead of an old one that I could only just afford. I'd started to explore new and exciting places and do things that I had never believed I would ever be able to do.

Whether you think you can,
or whether you think you can't,
You're right.

Henry Ford 1863 – 1947

Think about that. How many times in your life have you wanted to do something, but didn't think you could? Once you have done it, you realise that there was no reason why you couldn't do it in the first place.

It was only you limiting yourself.

I remember about 5 years ago I went into a car show-room to look at new cars. Up until that time I didn't go in, do you know why? Because, I didn't think that I was worthy! 'How can I with my low wage and overdraft, go and look at new cars?

Surely they will know that I cannot afford one, they'll just kick me out'. Honestly, that's where my mind was, I was a small-minded thinker.

As I leaned more and started to open my mind to the possibilities I became bolder and bolder. I went to the Nissan garage, and then I went to a Jaguar garage and one amazing day I went to the Austin Martin garage.

I don't know who was more terrified that day, my Daughter or I. In her book 'Feel The Fear And Do It Anyway', Susan Jeffers says that the only way to overcome fear is by doing it. So walking towards the Austin Martin show-room door, I ignored how I felt inside and kept on going.

When I got inside they were happy to see me. They treated me like any other potential customer. I'd broken my personal barrier. These days I'm happy to buy cars from dealerships. I'm happy to walk around the Ferrari or Lamborghini dealerships. I no longer have that fear.

Get out there and overcome your fears.

That is why, when my career took this wonderful up turn, I was ready for it. I took on the responsibilities that I had never previously had, and hadn't thought that I was capable of, and loved it. I bought myself an executive saloon. It didn't matter what other people thought; I was worthy of what I wanted.

This is one of the lessons; people will try and hold you back. Now that you have discovered 'The Secret', don't let that feeling of an abundant future slip from your fingers or be forced from your mind by other peoples ideas, thoughts or ideals.

You are worthy enough to have what ever you want out of this life. You can follow your dream.

There is an interesting fact, if there is a bucket full of crabs, as one reaches for the top the rest pull him back, people are very much the same. Everyone wants to see you do well, just so long as you are not doing better than them.

It's actually quite interesting, when you friends start passing negative comments about your recent achievements. When they aren't impressed with your new persona. That's when you know things are starting to work for you. They have the same choices that you do. If they chose to not follow you, that's their problem, not yours.

If you need to, buy them a copy of this book or 'The Secret'

When my friends start doing that I just pass them a copy of 'The Secret'. If they want to change something in their life they have to be prepared to change something in their life. Did I mention that before…..

Chapter 13

MANIFESTING

You may have noticed that I have read a number of books by some of the greatest people in the world. There is something I have to admit. In most of these books there are exercises for you to complete. Make a list of what you want, set out your goals for the next 5 years, make a 'today' list. I think I would have moved on, made more money, been happier with life sooner, if I had make these lists that all of these good people suggested.

I will state this very simply. If you do not write down your dreams, goals and ambitions, you will be very lucky for them to come true. Writing them down is unbelievably powerful. The usual excuse that most people come up with is, but as I'm reading book I haven't got a pen or paper at hand. Another popular one is 'I'm not sure where I left it…

I'll make this very clear, you can either have excuses or the future you want, the choice is yours. Let me give you a powerful example of how doing this produces results.

In his book 'How To Achieve Your Potential' Skip Ross relates the following story. There was a guy whose job was paying well, but also had a business outside of his daytime job, which was doing well too.

The business had been a struggle for a while but this guy had persisted. To help him keep his focus he was following his mentor's advice on visualising what he wanted, to help him do this he had a picture of his dream car. It was a Blue Ferrari; I forget what the model was.

He had this picture pinned up where he could see it every day.

Each and every day he would say to himself 'that's my car, that's my car'. As his business grew he got to the point where he could order his car.

A few weeks later he received a phone call from the Ferrari garage, his car had arrived but there was a slight problem, he had been sent the wrong colour, the car that he had been sent was in Ferrari Red. The Garage owner apologised for having the wrong car, would he like the red one? He thanked the garage owner for the phone call but said it was the blue one that he wanted. The garage owner apologised once again and said he would sort it out.

Another few weeks passed. The garage owner phoned again. He had received the guy's car, it was the right colour this time but there was another slight problem. It wasn't 100% new. This one had been used in display stands and promo work. This would obviously be reflected in the price and a further discount for the previous mess up. The guy went to look at the new car and discuss the price. It was exactly what he wanted and a nice price too with the discounts.

Being as proud as punch, he drove straight to work to show off his pride and joy to his colleagues. They all ooo'ed and ahh'ed at his new car. One of the guys said 'you got the car that you wanted'. 'Yes' said the guy. 'No' his colleague said, 'I don't think you understand'.

Dashing back into the office and returning a few moments later with the picture that had been on the guy's desk for the past few months. He said 'you have the car that you wanted, look'. He handed him the picture. The car that they guy had just bought was the one in the picture! ! ! !

Let me explain this fully

He's bought THE actual one. He got what he had dreamed day and night for.

Can you see how powerful 'The Secret' is, and the teachings from the great people you see in 'The Secret' and from what you are reading here.

When you read 'you need to do this' you do in now, not in the morning, not later, but now. If you want your dream car, house, relationship, lifestyle, …………… you need to do what we tell you.

The thing always happens
That you really believe in;
And the belief in a thing
makes it happen
Frank Lloyd Wright 1869-1959

Chapter 14

NEGATIVE PEOPLE

They are out there, they always will be, and they will never change. I have come across it numerous times in personal development books.

A positive thinker does not refuse to recognize
the negative,
He refuses to dwell on it.
Positive thinking is a form of thought which habitually
looks for the best results from the worst conditions.
Norman Vincent Peale 1898-1993

There are a couple of things to remember about negative people. Firstly they consider that they are right and for a lot of them, making you feel bad is there way of making them selves feel better.

There are two things that people do. Firstly they think that they are right and you are wrong and they want to make sure that you understand this. The truth is that you can actually both be right but that's a topic for another book.

The second reason why people do this is to prevent you from getting hurt. They don't want to see you fail. The interesting fact is that you should fail because through failure grows strength and character.

I know some people who have failed a lot but because they do so many things, some things work and it's those that put them where they are.

John Maxwell's book 'Fail Your Way To Success' goes into a lot of detail of this. If you have lot of things go wrong in your life, everything that you try fails, then read this book. It will give you the boost you need and help you realize that you are in very great company.

When I was a young man, I observed that
Nine out of ten things that I did were failures.
I didn't want to be a failure, so I did
ten times more work.
George Bernard Shaw 1856-1950

An incident happened recently where a friend and colleague of mine at work had a go at me for going on an all-inclusive holiday.

I was on a program to loose weight and get fit; he thought that with all of the food and drink being free on holiday, I'd eat and drink my way into increasing my weight.

I stood there and just looked at him. Here is a guy who hasn't been on holiday for about 10 years, whose last holiday was a 3-day break to Euro Disney, and he thinks he can tell what I am likely to be doing on my holiday.

True, on an all-inclusive holiday you can eat and drink too much, but there were two big differences between him and me. 1, This was my 10th all-inclusive holiday. I knew that although the food and drink is always available, I could just have what you want. 2, He didn't understand my determination to succeed at this program.

As it turned out, I did loose weight on that holiday. Admittedly it wasn't as much as I would have liked, but I know many people who can put on half a stone a week on all-inclusive holiday.

Let me give you another example of just how much someone else's opinion can be damaging to you. It will give you an idea about the influence that others can have.

In the 1970's McDonald's was just starting out. To increase their business they were offering franchises at very good discounts. A guy went to a meeting where the McDonald's corporation staff explained in detail why it was such a good opportunity, why it was such a trendsetter and how profitable it would be.

The guy was so impressed that he paid for 2 restaurants. I don't know what the exact figures were. Let's say $5,000 each. In 1970's money that was a substantial amount of money, but it's nothing compared to what you pay today for one.

The guy was so excited about what he had done, that he went back to his hometown and went to meet the guys in his usual bar. He then told them about his purchases. He explained to them what he could remember from the presentation.

His 'friends' then convinced him that no one would ever want to eat burgers out of polystyrene boxes, nor would anyone want to eat chips out of a cardboard box. His friends, who had no financial training or experience, assumed that they knew more than the people from McDonalds. They convinced him that he was making a big mistake. The following day he cancelled the cheque!

If he had kept the restaurants, how much money could he have made? Of the money that he lost, how much did his 'friends' give him back?

There is something important to remember, your friends won't pay your bills.

Opinions are like arse holes, everyone has one
Anonymous, obviously

IT IS NOT THE CRITIC WHO COUNTS

"It is not the critic who counts, not the one who points out how the strong man stumbled or how the doer of deeds might have done better.

The credit belongs to the man who is actually in the arena. Whose face is marred with sweat and dust and blood. Who strives valiantly, who errs and comes short again and again.

Who knows the great enthusiasms, the great devotions, and spends himself in a worthy cause. Who, if he wins, knows the triumph of high achievement; and who, if he fails, at least fails while daring greatly.

So that his place shall never be with those cold and timid souls who know neither victory or defeat."

Theodore Roosevelt, 26th US President 1858-1919

Chapter 15

WHO CAN DO IT?

There are two butts in life, the but that prevented you from doing something, and the Butt that you need to get off sometimes to go and do things.

What we all need in life is someone who helps us, to mentor us. Someone who is positive. In John Maxwell's book 'Fail Your Way To Success' John describes Walt Disney. Walt was a guy who, if he asked 100 people what they though of his idea if 97 disagreed and only 3 agreed, he'd do it.

If everyone is swimming down stream, it doesn't mean you have to follow them, swim up stream instead. Walt went bankrupt twice before he made it big.

So many people said to him 'who want's to watch a drawing of a mouse'!!!! 'There are already enough Theme Parks around, who's going to come to yours'? As we all know, Disney is huge.

Around here, however,
we don't look backwards for very long.
We keep moving forward,
opening up new doors and doing new things…
and curiosity keeps leading us down new paths."
Walt Disney 1901 – 1966

Another couple of people who are worth while looking at are Ross Perod and Bill Gates. Ross Perod worked for IBM who, in the 1970's, made computers. And as we all know computers are programmed and operated by computer programmers.

Ross's idea was to make computers easier to operate by making an interface, what we know today as software. He approached his employers, but they weren't interested. As they said, 'there is money in making computers, there is no money in software'!

He, and several of his colleagues, left IBM and set up their own company. As you can probably guess he made millions in his software business and IBM didn't. Incidentally Ross bought some wasteland in Texas with his profits.

This he developed, and it is (as far as I am aware) the biggest oil deposit in America. All because he had an idea and followed up on it regardless what other people thought.

We all know of Bill Gate's success with Microsoft. He again had an idea of moving the software from skilled and trained operatives and opening it up so that all of us, you and I, can operate and use computers.

So the thing to remember is this, **it's your opinion that counts the most**. Yes, listen to others but compare what they say with their qualifications and experience. Although doctors are highly educated and trained, you wouldn't take financial advice of your doctor just because he is clever.

Don't let your 'friends' and family grind you down. If you have got an idea that will change you, keep on going for it. Read other books that I have mentioned here. Don't take my word for anything, read what other successful people say.

Read from people who have been where you are and achieved the things in life that you want to. There is nothing better than having a successful person helping and mentoring you.

What is the difference between a friend and a mentor? A friend tells you what you want to hear, a mentor tells you what you need to hear.

Consider the postage stamp:
Its usefulness consists in the ability
To stick to one thing till it gets there.
Josh Billings 1818 – 1885

Chapter 14

POSITIVE SELF TALK

Positive self talk, what's that all about? The first time I heard of it I thought it was just some mumbo jumbo. As you tell people about it, the first thing that people will say is 'ah yes, that's brain washing'.

In some ways it is similar, but instead of getting you to do what you don't want to do, it helps you achieve what you want to achieve.

Let me give you a brief rundown of my understanding of self-talk. If you want to know more, then you should read Chad Helmstetter's book 'What To Say When You Talk To Your Self'.

Firstly there is something very important to know and understand about self-talk. That is, you already do it every day, and for most of the day.

The trouble is that most of the time, what you say to yourself is negative! Let me give you a couple of examples.

There are two guys stood outside a car show room, both are looking longingly at a brand new bright red sports car with all of the latest flash gadgets. One of the guys is thinking 'I'm going to have one, one day'. The second guy is thinking 'I could never afford one of those'.

Guess which one has most chance of getting one and

guess which one will never own one.

For the second example let me ask you a question, have you ever stepped off a curb onto a road without looking properly or walking into something that you shouldn't have and immediately thought 'I'm such an idiot'?

It's ok if you have, we all have the same thoughts and most importantly, you can't help the thoughts that pop into your mind.

What you can do, and where positive self talk comes in, is what you do next. If you have a negative thought 'I'm such an idiot' immediately say to yourself 'so what, I walked into it, I was too busy enjoying myself' or 'that was really funny'.

Don't keep on rerunning the moment in your mind while continuously telling yourself you are such an idiot. This is called Reinforcive Programming.

If you tell your self that you are an idiot enough times, guess what, you will become one.

Once we can reduce the number of negative comments going around our heads then we can really start to do some great work. Now we are going to reprogram our minds with everything we want and need out of life.

Here again we have to be careful how we say it. Instead of saying 'I want to loose some weight', we say 'I am loosing weight'. Instead of saying 'I want to attract a partner', say 'I am very attractive to the opposite sex'.

Always use the present tense and always state it in such a way that you have got what ever it is that you want. You're reprogramming your subconscious. Your subconscious believes what you tell it.

If you say you weight 10 stone, your subconscious will believe you. If you tell it every day that you weight 10 stone, then over a period of time, that is what you will weight.

I know it's wrong to lie, but your subconscious doesn't know if you are lying or not. Also if you tell your subconscious that you weight 10 stone and it realizes that you aren't, it will make changes within you until you do!

At the same time that you are reprogramming your mind you will also be using 'The Secret'.

I keep on saying that these changes take a time to arrive, to manifest. While that is true I will give you a couple of examples of how things can happen very quickly.

Can you possibly change your life by thought alone? No. Can you change your life by positive thought, intent and action? Read the following story and decide for your self.

I heard this story on Rock FM that is the local radio station for Preston in the UK. I think I heard it in 2010. This is a real story about a real person.

Joe was stood drinking in a bar one night enjoying a night out having a few pints. There was a guy stood next to him who looked all dejected. His shoulders were down and he was staring into his pint.

Curiosity got the better of Joe and he asked the guy what the problem was. It turns out that he'd promised his son a magician for his birthday and his wife had been bugging him to get it organized.

'That's not too bad' said Joe, 'there must be plenty in the phone book. When is your son's party?' Tomorrow, was the guys reply?

Now I must mention at this stage that Joe had been in the bar for a while, he'd consumed more than a couple of beers and he was not aware that his Dutch courage was about to come out of mouth.

Joe turns to face the guy and says 'no worries mate, it's your lucky night; I am actually a Children's entertainer and Magician'. The guy's face just lit up. He gave Joe the details of where the party was and agreed to pay Joe one hundred pound for the 2 hours work. The guy left happy with a lift in his stride.

Joe wandered back over to his friend who asked him who the guy was that he's been talking too. 'Oh him' says Joe 'I'm doing his son's Birthday party tomorrow and doing a magic show for him'. 'That's great' said his mate 'but there are a couple of problems. 1, You don't have kids and don't know how to handle them. 2, You have never run a kids party before, they'll eat you alive. 3, You're a Welder and have never done a magic trick in your life'.

'Minor point' said Joe 'I also told him that I would be doing party songs with my friend and his guitar, so you need to start practicing in the morning.

The following day Joe took the day off work, bought some magic tricks from a local toyshop and practiced for the rest of the day.

Joe and his friend did so well at that party that several of the parents there booked him for their children's parties. Within a couple of weeks both Joe and his friend quit their regular jobs and are having a great time entertaining children, earning more than they were before and enjoying life a lot.

There are several lessons to learn there.

1, When you come across an opportunity and it feels right, go for it, you never know what the outcome might be.

2, Be you are prepared to put in some extra work, you can change your life in some any ways that you could never imagine

3, As you change your life for the better, you can change other people's lives too.

The second story I want to tell you about is a nowhere near as life changing as that story, but it does prove how, when you think about it things do happen.

Yesterday I was walking around Wal-Mart with my Daughter doing a bit of weekend shopping. We stopped by the Coffee Makers. I'd been looking at the Tassimo systems for a while but I was undecided because I didn't know how good they really were.

We've all done the same thing, Bought a coffee maker, or some other 'Kitchen Appliance' that was great for the first week. Gathered dust for the next couple of weeks. Then spent the next year in a cupboard.

I've been there before and didn't really fancy spending a hundred Dollars on something that wouldn't get used.

Well, this morning at work (my day job) I got a team email inviting us to a free Bagel as one of the guys at work had just become a proud Dad. We all wandered over and had a chat with him.

As we were talking away, I noticed this coffee maker on the desk.

I'd looked at the Tassimo one the day before but also at a cheaper one that was half the price. Something inside me just wasn't comfortable so I'd walked away.

I started chatting to these two people who shared the coffee maker on their desk and they had nothing but praise for it. The next thing that he said was the important part. Wal-Mart, that week, was having a sale on them. They were 20 Dollars cheaper than normal. To cut a long story short. I bought one, extra Coffee and Hot Chocolate things to go in it and some 'Oh Henry's' (well, I just had to).

This is the really real cool thing. The total price I paid for everything was the same price of the coffee maker in our usual store.

Isn't it amazing?

Chapter 17

PUSHING THE EDGE OF THE ENVELOPE

A test pilot takes an aircraft to its limits in speed, height and maneuverability. They fly it from where it is known to be safe, to areas where they are unsure. It's called 'pushing the edge of the envelope'.

This is what we must do if we want to achieve new and interesting things in our lives.

As children we tend to do more things, we push the envelope.

Once we reach adulthood we sort of feel that we don't need to do anything new anymore. By the time we reach our 30's they have our routines that we are comfortable with. What actually happens is that you do less and less. You certainly don't try anything new.

'It's easier to do nothing new', is most people attitudes.

A friend of mine has been going regularly to the gym for at least the last 5 or 6 years. One of his favorite activities at the gym (apart from watching all of the ladies working hard) is the Aerobiking / Spinning classes.

As a youngster I'd ridden a bike for years too and from school. In fact I used to ride it every day, anywhere I needed to go. When I was younger I was comfortable on a bike. In more recent years I spent a year riding to work, as I couldn't afford to run a car on the road.

That year I clocked up over 1,000 miles.

As I got older, and bigger, a bike didn't look such a good prospect. I preferred bikes with big engines. Anyway, back to the story. My friend Dave kept on saying that I should start doing spinning classes.

I wasn't convinced. I found out that one of the friendly instructors at my Gym was doing the spinning class so I booked myself in for it. On the night of my first aerobiking session there was only me booked in for the class, this suited me down to the ground. Just after we had got settled on the bike the instructor calls in a guy that he knew, he'd never been on an aerobike either.

We then did a full half an hour training session. I have to admit, that it's one of the hardest things that I have ever done. The effort you put it is totally up to you but following the Instructors guidance, we did what I thought, was a fairly reasonable training session.

How did I feel afterward, totally knackered. By the time I left the gym I'd recovered enough to book myself in for the following week.

If people are prepared to take the action,
the opportunities are waiting for them.
Simon 'Amazing' Clarke

Try new things, because once you start pushing the edge of your personal envelope, there will be no stopping you. Again, it doesn't happen over night, but little by little you will accept new things and actually enjoy challenges.

I'll tell you something that I have found. You come back from doing something new, something that you have been looking forward to for the last few weeks.

It's only when you sit down and think about it later that you suddenly realize that a year ago, you would have never considered doing something so way outside of your comfort zone.

That's when you realize that you are on the journey.

Chapter 18

THE COSMIC ORDERING SERVICE

First things first, as I mentioned in the introduction I think it has been my lack of focus that has held me back in the past. Without a clear vision for the future, it is difficult to have the future that I want. I'd like to relate here a story that that I came across a few years ago. It's from this that I get most of my inspiration.

An Earthling died and went to heaven; heaven was a truly wondrous place where the Earthling was met by a group of wonderful Angels. The Angels helped the Earthling settle in and showed them the wonderful thing that Heaven has to offer a mere mortal.

Heaven consisted of a corridor with doors on either side. The Angels approached each door excitedly and showed the Earthling all of the wonderful things that the heavenly world held. After a short while the Earthling notices that the Angels were taking him to many different rooms but noticed that there was one door that the Angels would go quiet as they went past and would never enter.

The Earthling asked what was in the room. The Angels went quiet and one answered saying that although they couldn't stop the Earthling from entering, it was a room that they didn't want to show them. The Earthling was curious so decided to enter the room.

When he entered he found a place of such wonders.

There was a magnificent house set in many acres with a great swimming pool. There were amazing friends at this house. He spotted a beautiful and charming Lady that he knew was his wife. There were luxury cars of all types and images of exotic locations from all around the world. The Earthling was totally awed by the room while the Angels were still and quiet.

A little confused the Earthling asked the Angels what the room was and why he hadn't been shown the room before. One Angel approached them and said quietly, 'these are all of the things that God had planned for you, but you didn't think that you were worthy of.

Ask you're self-this question, do you have in your life all of the things that you think God has planned for you?

I know I haven't. There is so much more out there for each of us, all we have to do is ask. It's like Aladdin and the Magic lamp. All you have to do is to ask the Genie for it. One difference thought between Aladdin and us, is that we don't get three wishes.

We don't have a limit.

A man is what he thinks about
All day long
Ralph Waldo Emerson 1803 – 1882

So how do we get something that we wish for and bring it into our lives? We write it down as a goal and think about it every day. Our subconscious brings things into our lives that slowly change us from where we are to where we want to be. There are many great books out there that you can read on this.

There is the 'Aladdin Factor' and 'How To Get From Where You Are, To Where You Want To Be' by Jack Canfield. Both of these books require not only to be read, but also for you to act upon what you read. It is the doing part that is important, not the reading.

Tip – The sooner you write your goals, the sooner they can start to become in your life.

> *The happiest people seem to be those*
> *Who are producing something;*
> *The bored people are those who are consuming much*
> *and producing nothing.*
> William Inge 1860 – 1954

I certainly understand the lady in the next story. I can't remember where I read or heard this story but it is amazing.

She was doing ok in her job, but it wasn't what she wanted to do. Her dream was to have her own business. She had the ideas but she didn't have the money to set up the business and she needed money to live on while she got the business going.

To get her away from her current job and set up her business she decides that she needs $100,000. Although she had her own idea's, she decided to ask her friends what they thought was an easy way to make that sort of money.

Most of her friends came back saying that they thought she could make that sort of money if she wrote a book.

'Great', she thought, 'I'll write a book, but what sort of books sell really well?'

Again she went around all of her friends. They all came back with similar answers, a book of cooking recipes.

'Brilliant', she thought, 'but I've only got a couple of my own'.

She asked her friends for their favorite recipes, put them together in a book and found a publisher to sell her book.

She made the $100,000 that she wanted to and quit her job.

Fortunately in this case, lots of her friends were positive and were willing to help. There are a lot of helpful people out there. Just be careful of the negative people that I have described before.

I remember a few years ago a friend of mine got together with a wonderful lady. They were both adventurous. They went on holiday to Central America. As part of their stay they climbed a mountain and camped over night on the high plateau. When the sun arose in the morning to reveal the clear blue sky, they looked down and could see the Panama Canal, the Atlantic Ocean and the Pacific Ocean. I thought too myself when they told me, what a truly wonderful experience to share.

Is that the sort of experience that you would like to share?

Life is not measured by the number of breaths we take,
but by the moments that take our breath away
Unknown

Chapter 19

ACTION PLAN FOR YOUR FUTURE

Where do you go from here? What should you do next?

You have probably noticed throughout this book that there is a reoccurring theme.

It's up to you to do what ever you want to do for your Future.

Rule 1, you are 100% Responsible for your life.
                                              Jack Canfield

You are a clever person. You also have a desire, but at this moment in time you do not have the knowledge that you need to grow.

Here are the books that I recommend that everyone should read.

This is assuming that by now you have finally watched / read or listened to The Secret'.

I've mentioned these books already but just to give you a short list.

'How To Get From Where You Are To Where You Want To Be' - Jack Canfield

'Feel The Fear And Do It Any way' – Susan Jeffers

'Fail Your Way To Success' – John Maxwell
'Rich Dad, Poor Dad' – Robert Kiyosaki
'You've Got To Read This Book' – Jack Canfield
'Write it down and make it happen' – Henriette Klauser

These books are all have different messages and things for you to learn. They will give you a good grounding and a great head start.

After that it's really up to you to follow your path. Most of the books above quote other books. I've read books from books or Authors mentioned in the books that I have read. You will find your path.

Audio books are great too. Especially if you have a long commute to work, or have a job where you can listen to an MP3 player.

Use your car like a mobile University.

With Internet sites like YouTube, there are a great many ways to see people live and hear their message.

There is nothing better than going to a Seminar, especially if there are multiple speakers. To be in a room full of people, who are thinking like you, wanting the same as you and who are prepared to take control of their lives.

What does the future hold for you?
Anything you want it too.
Simon 'Amazing' Clarke

I love positive people. Actually, I've just joined Toastmasters. There will be a Toastmasters club in your area.

They are positive, friendly people who were all once shy. They are there to help you.

> *Don't wait for the light to appear*
> *At the end of the tunnel,*
> *Stride down there*
> *And light the bloody thing yourself*
>
> Sara Henderson 1936-2005

In my next book you will be able to read more specific details of how to change you life. It is a more in depth look at your next steps.

I'll also explain why teamwork is the key. You need to mix and mingle with like-minded groups of upwardly mobile people. Find a mastermind club in your area, or create your own.

I will also explain what tithing is and why giving away things to help others will help you so much.

For now I wish you all of the success that you are prepared to work for.

> *Go confidently in the direction of your dreams*
> *Live the life you've imagined*
>
> Henry David Thoreau 1817-1862

POST SCRIPT

A lot of the quotes in my book were taken from 'The Complete Pocket Positives An Anthology Of Inspired Thoughts' compiled by Maggie Pinkney.

Others are mine, or ones that I remember but can't remember where from.

I mention several Authors and their books in my Book; here are their personal Web sites

Use the your usual Internet search engines to find their books that I have mentioned e.g. Google, Amazon, eBay etc.

The Secret	thesecret.tv
Jack Canfield	www.jackcanfield.com
Neale Donald Walshe	www.nealedonaldwalsch.com
James Arthur Ray	www.jamesray.com
Susan Jeffers	www.susanjeffers.com
David Schwartz	davidjschwartz.com
Joe Vitale	www.mrfire.com
Bob Doyle	www.meetbobdoyle.com
Bob Proctor	www.bobproctor.com
Chad Helmstetter	www.shadhelmstetter.com
Henriette Klauser	www.henrietteklauser.com
Mind Movies	www.mindmovies.com
Robert Kiyosaki	www.richdadcoaching.com
John Maxwell	www.johnmaxwell.com

www.ingramcontent.com/pod-product-compliance
Lightning Source LLC
Chambersburg PA
CBHW071956070426
42453CB00008BA/902